Tom and Pop

by Michael P. Fertig
illustrated by Kersti Frigell

Practice Decodable 15

McGraw Hill Education

Bothell, WA • Chicago, IL • Columbus, OH • New York, NY

MHEonline.com

Send all inquiries to:
McGraw-Hill Education
8787 Orion Place
Columbus, OH 43240

ISBN: 978-0-02-132669-3
MHID: 0-02-132669-X

Printed in the United States of America.

7 8 9 CTM 23

Tom is hot.

Tom hops in a pond.

A pond is not hot.

Pop hops on land.

Pop has a pot on top.

Tom is not hot.

Pop is not hot.